CW00517413

boys
with
beer

A stage play in three acts

by Paul Boakye

Published by Paul Boakye Associates (2019).

Contents

Title   1

Copyright   3

Characters   5

Introduction   6

Act One   14

Act Two   47

Act Three   63

Afterword   89

Copyright

condition being imposed on the subsequent purchaser.

PUBLICATION: *Boy with Beer* was first published in Great Britain in "Black Plays: 3," edited by Yvonne Brewster (1995) by **Methuen Drama** an imprint of Reed Consumer Books Ltd.

Also published by Alexander Street Press in the United States of America for an academic audience (2003).

ISBN: 978-0-9935389-1-9

ISBN 978-0-9935389-1-9

9 780993 538919 >

Characters

Boy with Beer was first presented by
House of Boache Productions, in
association with This is Now Theatre
Company, at The Man in the Moon
Theatre, London, from 14th January to 1st
February 1992, with the following cast:

KARL,
Ghanaian, 27   *CLIVE*
                          WEDDERBURN

DONOVAN,
Afro-Caribbean, 21   *TUNDE OBA*

Directed by   *Steven Luckie*

Designed by   *John Lynch*

Lighting by   *Nicola*
                          Stammers

Sound by   *Jimmy Mackness*

Produced by   *Paul Boakye*
                      and Steven Luckie

The action takes place in a London flat on
two levels.

Introduction

Back in the early eighties when I was learning to read for pleasure because the lives of Black people were not reflected on British TV, I would recite *The politics of rich painters* and other similar poetry to any and everybody who cared to listen. A few years later, when I first started to write no wonder, my thoughts were filled with the language and imagery of Amiri Baraka and the "agitprop" tones of the Black Power Movement. To my family, friends, and colleagues in our part of multi-racial London, I was generally considered a very angry young man. "Too Black, too out-spoken, too political, offensive." It didn't help that I couldn't relate to any concept of "Black Power" lacking an economic base, nor that I was in a "mixed-race" relationship at the time, both of which only served to propel my anger at the world and fuel a sense of self-loathing. Amiri Baraka had introduced me to the possibility of writing "Black," and at the same time writing anything I wanted to (even that which other Black people may not understand or embrace). Blackness was not formulaic, but was it universal? In hindsight, however, I know now that I was writing from a restrictive position of opposition to the world and myself.

James Baldwin's *Giovanni's Room* was the first book I read by a Black author. It may well have been a subconscious inspiration for the play *Boy with Beer*, but at the time, I found the whole novel sombre and very depressing. Yet, that didn't prevent me seeking out other available titles by Baldwin within a 10-mile radius of my local library. I already knew the works of Shakespeare, Dickens, and even Mark Twain, now I was hungry to see the contemporary world through the eyes of others that looked more like me. Jimmy served this purpose to a certain extent, but I could not warm to his sentimentality or the overtly religious sermonising of his novels, that is until I read *Just Above My Head*. That book opened a lot in me because it was so full of love and passions. That's when I started thinking. Up until that point, I was used to reading and writing so much about people who despise us that my priorities had become a bit jaded. *Just Above My Head* was like walking into a Black community and opening the door to a whole other world where wild things happen, but there is still so much devotion. Before then, my heart had been filled with anger and pain at the "motion of history" as Baraka puts it, but now my characters could live.

When I wrote *Boy with Beer* in 1991, I didn't know what I was doing. My best friend Derek St. Louis had just died suddenly of an AIDS-related illness, and I knew that I wanted to commemorate his life, but beyond that, I had only some vague idea of taking the concept of self-love to its conclusion. With some plays, you know exactly what you want to say, and with others, it's a case of opening up your mind to allow what comes to come from beyond your own direct experience or knowledge. This is the essential difference between *Wicked Games* and *Boy with Beer*. The former came out of a real trip to Ghana, and the latter just evolved. I remember sitting down to draft the first scenes between Karl and Donovan after coming back from the theatre with Black filmmaker and director Topher Campbell. He had invited me to see a gay play by a white writer, and at the end of the production, he turned to me and said, "That was crap. You could write better than that!" I thought, "bloody cheek!" I went home immediately, sat down, and wrote the first act. I fell asleep at the computer, woke up later, looked at what I'd written and thought - "What the hell is this?" It wasn't until I showed it to a group of friends, triggering a massive discussion, that I realised what I had done. "But can you write another 30 or 40 pages," they kept on asking, "this is not the end?" Never one to miss a challenge, I thought I'd give it a go.

I had always been attracted to the works of Toni Morrison; I just couldn't read her novels. I would get through thirty or so pages, but just don't ask me what it was all about! I must have struggled with *The Bluest Eye* for years before I finally gave up and decided to read something completely different. Dad had always talked about Ghana, and I naturally turned to Ayi Kwei Armah's *The Healers* and *2000 Seasons* when dad died in 1984. I had never heard of Jungian Psychology, so when I finished these two books, I thought that I had discovered the term "Collective Consciousness." I found out later that Jung's great achievement was to explain how the unconscious could be accessed through mythology and archetypes, and Armah had certainly accessed my unconscious with his vision of reciprocity and unity. I kept thinking as I read, "I know this...I know this. This is so familiar." Thereafter, reading Toni Morrison was a breeze, I started with *Beloved,* and everything fell into place. In fact, I now craved elements of the wild and magical in all fiction, and I just had to write for public consumption.

No prizes for guessing that writing for film and television was my first choice (many people say they can detect this from my writing style), but since this area of the industry was already sewn-up, theatre seemed a more realistic option. Yet most theatre professionals will tell you that "Black people don't go to the theatre in England," and even as I write this, our one Black theatre company, Talawa, doesn't own a building, has to rely on co-productions, and apologises for only accepting material from Black writers.

"I'm ashamed to observe that we lost many opportunities for what is called colour-blind casting. We even staged plays about young Londoners and one about the merchant Navy with a cast of twenty and managed to have no Black actors in them. That wasn't even realistic for British life at the time, let alone progressive for out theatre policy. Such narrowness of mind was the result of a middle-aged director like myself and all the White guest directors we employed at the time casting principally from actors they know, and from their minds running along "conventional," meaning White, lines." – Philip Hedley, Artistic Director of Britain's Theatre Royal Stratford East in his essay, *A Theatre Director's Journey to the Obvious."*

The Theatre Royal Stratford East was among the first places I sent the finished *Boy with Beer* script, but the various rejection letters spoke of "pornographic," "lewd," and "unworkable," so I decided to produce it myself. Many prominent theatre directors were among the first-row audience, and the play has been produced several times since (although a screenplay continues to languish in a drawer somewhere).

I started to write because the lives of Black people were not being portrayed on British stage and screen. Although there have been some improvements lately with the inclusion of Black characters in mainstream television programming, it is still rare to see Black life at the centre of serious drama in England. In this respect, I owe a debt of gratitude to the

Internet in its ability to bypass traditional borders and barriers in bringing the work of Black writers and artists to the attention of wider audiences.

Paul Boakye
London, June 2001

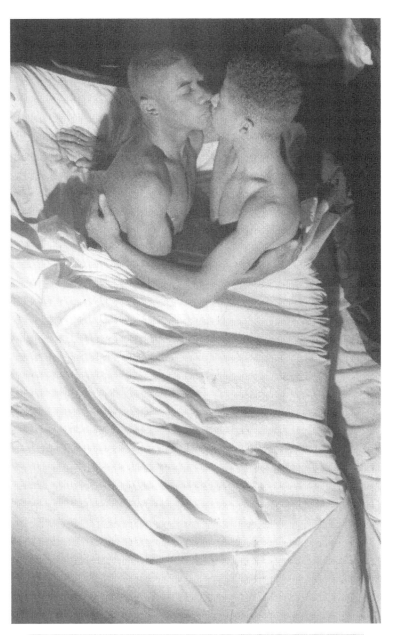

Act One

A kitchen-dining room. KARL frantically prepares dinner for two. He sets the table, lights an incense stick, and puts on "LOVING PAUPER" by Gregory Isaacs. The doorbell rings. He panics and runs to the door:

KARL:	Donovan? Hi! Come in.
DONOVAN:	This place is hard to find.
KARL:	Come in. It's not numbered properly.
DONOVAN:	Went right past it at first.
KARL:	It says thirty-five upstairs. People don't notice there's a thirty-five-A down here. Pass your coat. Ta. Go in. Grab a seat.
DONOVAN:	So that's what you look like.
KARL:	And that's what you look like. *(Silence)* What's in the bag?
DONOVAN:	I got some beer on the way.
KARL:	Cheers. Do you want one-a-these now?
DONOVAN:	Might as well. *(Silence)* What's that smell? Have you

| | cooked? You haven't cooked, have you? I couldn't eat a thing. |
| **KARL:** | No problem. |

KARL, clearly disappointed, removes cutlery from the table.

	Did you have a nice Christmas?
DONOVAN:	Christmas is boring, man.
KARL:	Let's hope the New Year gets better.
DONOVAN:	I'm looking forward to summer this year, though, man. People are bubbling in the summer.

Silence. DONOVAN coughs.

KARL:	What do you do? You said you were phoning from work. What do you do?
DONOVAN:	I wasn't phoning from work. I was phoning from round some girl's.
KARL:	No. The first time. You said you were phoning from work.
DONOVAN:	Oh, then.
KARL:	What do you do?
DONOVAN:	I drive.
KARL:	Mini cabs?

DONOVAN:	I drive a van for this building firm.
KARL:	Right.
DONOVAN:	So you live here on your own, do you?
KARL:	Yeah. What about you?
DONOVAN:	I live with a friend. Not too far from here.
KARL:	What sort of friend?
DONOVAN:	A good friend.
KARL:	How good is good? I mean, do you...
DONOVAN:	What, sex? Sometimes. Depends on the mood. Nothing much these days, cos she's going through a bad patch.
KARL:	So you're living with a woman?
DONOVAN:	I'm with her, yeah, cos she's going through a bad patch.
KARL:	Well, that's a shame.
DONOVAN:	I been there a year. She kind-a-needs me, y'know.
KARL:	We all need someone.
DONOVAN:	That's it, ennit. But it's petering out now our relationship, petering out. There's always a weak one, ain't there. You just gotta hold them up. That's what I'm doing. She's very good-looking. That's what all my mates say, anyway.

KARL:	They're the ones you got to watch.
DONOVAN:	You'd like her.
KARL:	You should have invited her round, Donovan.
DONOVAN:	I can ring her if you want.

KARL gives him a "you're very funny" look.
DONOVAN walks around the room - like a burglar casing the joint.

	This is a nice place you got here.
KARL:	It's not bad. *(Opens a beer)* Do you want this in the can or a glass?
DONOVAN:	You could have some raves here, man.
KARL:	Raves?
DONOVAN:	Yeah, you could have some wicked parties here.
KARL:	I'm thinking of having a party.
DONOVAN:	Do you do Hard-core?
KARL:	The porno or the music?
DONOVAN:	Parties, man, parties.
KARL:	Not lately.
DONOVAN:	They still have 'em, you know. Contortions, Rumours, and all them. Don't you go to none-a-them?
KARL:	Never heard of them.

DONOVAN: They still have 'em, man. Sussex, Surrey, Aldershot...them kind-a-places.

KARL: They move about?

DONOVAN: Every time.

KARL: Sounds like too much hard work to me.

DONOVAN: Madness, ennit. There's this place up in Dalston. Reggae place called Scandals. Doesn't open 'til seven in the morning. What you do is you go out to other places first. Get home for about five. Get a couple hours sleep. Get up, have a shower, something to eat, and get down there before the queues start up. That's a nice place Scandals. But you get tired, though, man. (Coughs. Takes a swig) That club last night...I was buzzing, you know, in that club last night.

KARL: Me too.

DONOVAN: I got this chest infection, right, so I don't smoke. That Bluenote Club, man, it was hot and sweaty and full-up-a-ganja smoke. It was giving me a buzz but it was getting in my eyes. I couldn't breathe. The club never had

	no air-conditioning. They should do something about that.
KARL:	How many clubs have air-conditioning?
DONOVAN:	Some have holes in the roof.
KARL:	I'll take your word for it.

<u>Silence. DONOVAN drinks and watches old reruns of Dame Edna on the television.</u>

DONOVAN:	She's good ain't she. What's here name again? Possum?
KARL:	You're into Dame Edna?
DONOVAN:	I wanna see this later. Saw it last week. She's good, man. She's a man, ain't she?
KARL:	Probably.
DONOVAN:	In twenty minutes. Okay. I wanna watch that. *(Drinks)* What did my friend say to you last night?
KARL:	He asked if the guy I was with was my boyfriend, as he put it. I said, "No, he's a friend." He said that his friend liked me and his friend wanted to know if he could talk to me. I told him I talk to anyone.
DONOVAN:	He's out of order, man.
KARL:	Why, wasn't he following

	your instructions?
DONOVAN:	I never said nothing to him.
KARL:	I thought you two were a regular double act.
DONOVAN:	Naw, man. Sometimes. Sometimes when I'm shy.
KARL:	You, shy?
DONOVAN:	Yeah, man.
KARL:	You don't seem shy to me.
DONOVAN:	And sometimes we mess about - chat people up for fun.
KARL:	For fun?
DONOVAN:	Yeah, you know, flirting.
KARL:	So you're a big flirt, are you?
DONOVAN:	Yeah.
KARL:	Do you flirt at your parties? Your Hardcore parties?
DONOVAN:	I flirt with everyone, man. It's packed, ennit. You have to flirt with them jus' to get 'em out've your way. Hardcore's brilliant. You're just dancing there. Everybody doing their own thing. Moving their arms about like this. Wild, man, wild. The girls are just tripping and wriggling their arms in-front-a-your face like inviting you for a fuck. Then there's the boys. I love white boys at Hardcore, man. They'll do anything for you. Share their joints...their

Es...their girls...even give you a lift right back to your own front door. Man, I mean, them white boys are so fucking good - I just love 'em. Step on a Black guy's toe, you could be dead within seconds, step on a white geezer's foot, he'll want to buy you a drink.

<u>KARL laughs.</u>

No, serious! The other night, right, I was pushing through this crowd. Where was I? - can't remember - anyway, I was pushing through this crowd. Split beer all down this white guy's shirt. I mean, all the beer, all over him. The guy turned round smiled, "Don't worry about a thing, mate, naw it's auright. It's wet enuff in 'ere as it is." Big grin across his face like this. Brushed it off. Just carried on dancing. I couldn't believe it. I wouldn't-a-done that, would you? I would-a-brushed it off, but I wouldn't-a-smiled about it. I would-a-said, "That's auright, mate, just make fucking sure you

don't do it again, auright
cunt!?"

**KARL looks at him
disapprovingly.**

Well? What would you-a-
done? Tell me something
about yourself. I'm well and
truly tired, man, but I'm a
good listener.

**DONOVAN sits back in
his chair, balancing on
the two back legs.**

	Come on then?
KARL:	I'm twenty-seven. I smoke a lot. I take photographs, and I live here.
DONOVAN:	Did you tell me about you took photographs last night?
KARL:	We didn't get that deep.
DONOVAN:	I can't remember what I said to you, you know. I'm so fucking tired as well. I feel like shit crawling. I was fresh before I got here.

**DONOVAN yawns, sits
down on a piece of paper,
pulls it from under him
and reads it.**

What's this, is this a love letter?

KARL: No, give it here, that's private.

DONOVAN: No, wait a minute, man, what's this?

(Reading) "We are not a people of yesterday. Ask when first a Brother's lips kissed a Brother's mouth." What's this? "We are not a people of the destroyer's world, our roots return to Anoa."

KARL: So you can read.

DONOVAN: I ain't an idiot, you know.

(Reading) "There by the banks of the sacred Pra we met. Before Ghana became just a distant memory. Before the desert became desert."

Wait, wait a minute, man!

(Reading) "In that fabulous Black time when Poets among us still sang songs of praise to the spirit of Brotherhood holding our people together."

KARL: You're taking the piss.

DONOVAN: No, I'm not. Let me finish.

(Reading) "Under the shade of a young Nim tree we slept, while the Prophet Densua pictured a time: The destroyer's would come; nail our soul to humiliation and hurl our benevolent ways into defeat and obscurity; where now in dream or awake, I think of you."

What's this? You don't write poetry, do you?

KARL: What do you think?

KARL snatches the poem. DONOVAN laughs and swigs beer.

DONOVAN: Naw, man, you should try writing songs. Then you could chat a thing or two about Africa.

KARL: And you know all about Africa?

DONOVAN: Did I say that? I didn't say that, did I? I know a thing or two about Rastas, but I didn't say I know anything about Africa, did I? Are you African?

KARL: Ghanaian.

DONOVAN:	What?
KARL:	I was born in Ghana, West Africa. I came here nine years ago to study.
DONOVAN:	I thought you was African.
KARL:	Is that a problem?
DONOVAN:	No, man, no, why?
KARL:	Only Africans and West Indians...
DONOVAN:	Ain't s'ppose to get on. I know, that's what people say.
KARL:	Doesn't mean it has to be that way.
DONOVAN:	*(Flinches. Changes the subject)* There's a party tonight.
KARL:	Oh, yeah?
DONOVAN:	There was a guy last night giving out invitations. Didn't he give you one?
KARL:	All I've got is this.
DONOVAN:	It was on a small piece of white paper.
KARL:	Unless it's in my coat pocket. Look, are you staying or going?
DONOVAN:	I'm s'ppose to page my friend. I'm so tired, though, man. I wanna relax a bit. Aaaaahhhhhh. Had two hours sleep last night. Woke up at five this morning. Driving some stuff up town. You get really worked up

with the roads so full.

**<u>Silence, DONOVAN
suddenly laughs out
loud.</u>**

	You was doing some really weird dancing last night in that club.
KARL:	Stoned outta my head and enjoying the music.
DONOVAN:	You was doing some really weird weird dancing, man. Your legs look like the Rubber Band Man's. *(Giggles)* Bending down, you were. Way, way, down as well. You was dancing right in-front-a-me.
KARL:	I didn't see you.
DONOVAN:	I was watching you. I said to myself ...Aaah... yeah, man...that's nice! Then all of a sudden, you just grab your drink and went. I thought - he'll come back.
KARL:	I didn't notice you.
DONOVAN:	I was right behind you.
KARL:	I didn't see you until you said hello.
DONOVAN:	That guy you were with?
KARL:	Mark?
DONOVAN:	He was clinging.
	Mark's my good mate. I like

Mark a lot. He has his faults. Don't we all. He's white...yeah...but he's a better friend to me than many Black guys have been.

DONOVAN: *(Takes a swig)* So what's happenin'?

KARL: What do you mean?

DONOVAN: What's happenin' now?

KARL: Nothing, by the looks of it.

DONOVAN: Are you fit?

KARL: *(On edge)* What kind of question is that?

DONOVAN: Are you fit?

KARL: Fit enough.

DONOVAN: How fit are you?

KARL: Right now? About as fit as I need to be.

DONOVAN: D'you reckon?

KARL: Have you got something in mind?

DONOVAN: I like to be blunt about these things.

KARL: Go ahead.

DONOVAN: Are you gonna give it to me tonight?

KARL: Is that what you want?

DONOVAN: Yeah.

KARL: Are you going somewhere special in a hurry? You've bought all this beer. We've got all night. What's the hurry?

DONOVAN: I didn't mean right-right

now.

KARL:	But you'd like to hit the sack soon?
DONOVAN:	No, no, not at all now.
KARL:	Have another beer. Wait for Dame Edna.
DONOVAN:	Might as well.
KARL:	Nothing better to do.

<u>DONOVAN goes to the fridge and takes another beer, he crosses to the window and looks out at the rain.</u>

DONOVAN:	You remind me of that singer.
KARL:	What singer?
DONOVAN:	Cockroach.
KARL:	Roachford.
DONOVAN:	*(Laughing)* I said, Cockroach, didn't I?
KARL:	Similar.
DONOVAN:	Roachford.
KARL:	I'm sexier than he is, though.
DONOVAN:	You're what?
KARL:	Sexier than he is.
DONOVAN:	How do you work that one out?
KARL:	I don't think he's sexy. He tries to be. But he could learn a thing or two from Seal.
DONOVAN:	You think Seal's sexy?
KARL:	Linford Christie is sexy.

DONOVAN: Would you admit to another Black man that you thought he was sexy?

KARL: Why not?

DONOVAN: No, man! *(Laughs)* You go out with a lot of white guys, don't you?

KARL: I have white friends.

DONOVAN: And your boyfriend now - he's white?

KARL: No. I've slept with white men, if that's what you want to know. But I want relationships with Black men.

DONOVAN: Yeah?

KARL: Yeah.

DONOVAN: I don't check for white people at all.

KARL: Your girlfriend is Black?

DONOVAN: Susan? Your colour.

KARL: That's good.

DONOVAN: She's a little joker Susan is. She makes me laugh.

KARL: That's nice to hear.

DONOVAN: She ain't too well right now.

KARL: What's wrong with her?

DONOVAN: Just woman problems, I s'ppose. I dunno. I mean, she's fit an' everything. It's jus' if it ain't one thing with her it's the other.

KARL: So does she know about you?

DONOVAN: No way, man. You joking!

	You couldn't tell a girl that you go with men. Unless the girl was a lesbian.
KARL:	Some couples work it out.
DONOVAN:	Some white couples work it out.
KARL:	But not you and your Susan?
DONOVAN:	I don't see how the relationship could work.
KARL:	So you lie to Susan instead?
DONOVAN:	I tell her what she needs to know. What else you gonna do? You ain't exactly gonna go up to her "Excuse me, babes, but I fuck men - hope you don't mind."
KARL:	Is that what you do?
DONOVAN:	All the time.
KARL:	There's a problem.
DONOVAN:	What's that?
KARL:	I want to make love to you too.
DONOVAN:	*(Shakes his head)* Uh-huh, man! Not possible!
KARL:	That's a big problem then.
DONOVAN:	That's why two bulls can't get laid.
KARL:	Sorry?
DONOVAN:	Why two men can't get it together.
KARL:	So what are the men you fuck?
DONOVAN:	Don't get me wrong...
KARL:	No! I think I know exactly

where you're coming from. Don't get me wrong! I enjoy a good fuck, and I give as good as I get. What makes you think that the men you fuck are any less than other men? And what would you know about it anyway?

DONOVAN: I didn't mean it like that. I don't know why I said it. Do you think I'm out of order? I'm out of order, 'en I? I know I am. So what are you saying?

KARL: I'm saying I don't sleep with men who have a problem turning over.

DONOVAN: So what are you saying?

KARL: I want your arse too.

DONOVAN: What - in the same night?

KARL: No big deal!

DONOVAN: We'll see how it goes.

KARL: We'll see how it goes before you fall asleep.

DONOVAN: Who's gonna fall asleep? *(Swigs)* Do you take Poppers?

KARL: I don't have any.

DONOVAN: Good thing a brought some then.

KARL: You've got a bottle with you?

DONOVAN: In my jacket pocket.

KARL: Whatever turns you on.

DONOVAN: Drink some more wine.

<u>DONOVAN pours KARL a glass of red wine.</u>

Red wine is good for you, anyway. Lots of iron.

KARL: Red is my favourite.

DONOVAN: I've never developed a taste for red wine. Can't stand the stuff really. Champagne is nice, though. You can get dead pissed on Champagne. No headaches, no hangovers, no nothing. I used to work in this Off-license in Peckham. Me and the landlady used to get pissed all the time on Champagne. Then she'd tempt me round the back with a fiver in her bra. I was only a kid, but she'd get me to give her one on the cold stone floor. Sometimes, if I was really good at it, she'd give me a tenner.

KARL: *(Teasing him)* Are you any good at it then?

DONOVAN: I think I am.

KARL: There's a big difference...

DONOVAN: What - thinking?

KARL: Between being good at it and thinking you're good at it. They're not always the same thing.

	There's only one way to find out. Try it!
KARL:	*(Flirting)* Is that a challenge or a boast?
DONOVAN:	There's only one way to find out.
KARL:	The bed's upstairs.
DONOVAN:	What kind of bed is it? Is it a comfortable bed?
KARL:	There's only one way to find out.
DONOVAN:	Maybe I should go up and test the bed. Bounce on it a bit. What do you think?

<u>KARL leads the way to the bedroom. Hanging from the walls are several black and white photographs of Black men in various stages of undress.</u>

	This is a nice bed. This is a nice room, man. Don't tell me, you're into wood. Are you a YUPPIE?
KARL:	Are you stupid?
DONOVAN:	Don't call me stupid! *(Testing bed)* This is a nice bed. Let's have a look at your pictures. Is this your boyfriend?
KARL:	Was.

DONOVAN:	*(Looking at photos)* He's nice. He looks very...hmmm...This is nice.
KARL:	That guy has got a beautiful arse.
DONOVAN:	I'm gonna have forty winks. Do you mind?
KARL:	I thought you wanted to watch Dame Edna?
DONOVAN:	That's in twenty minutes, man. I'll just rest for twenty minutes. Wake me up. Is there a T.V. up here?
KARL:	The television's downstairs.
DONOVAN:	I'm tired, you know.
KARL:	Take your clothes off.
DONOVAN:	If I take my clothes off, I'll only want to make love to you. You take yours off.
KARL:	If I take my clothes off, I'll only want to make love to you.
DONOVAN:	You're being silly. You're being very silly now.
KARL:	I think we both are.

<u>KARL removes DONOVAN's shoes.</u>

	Shall I turn the television off downstairs and bring everything up?
DONOVAN:	Might as well.
KARL:	Well, don't sound too eager.

You might ruin your street cred!

DONOVAN: I'm tired.

KARL: You must have known that before you got here.

DONOVAN: I know.

KARL: *(Annoyed)* I'm going downstairs to roll another joint. I forget you don't smoke.

DONOVAN: Look in my jacket pocket, bring the poppers up, will you.

DONOVAN closes his eyes and begins to snore. KARL enters and sits on the bed to roll a joint. He leans forward and kisses DONOVAN hard on the mouth.

What's happenin'?

KARL: You were about to take your clothes off.

DONOVAN jumps up, undresses, and gets back into bed in his underpants. He fumbles under the covers, removes his underpants, and throws them out onto the floor.

Progress! How much more of that can you handle in one night?

DONOVAN sucks his teeth. KARL removes condoms from a bowl and throws a few at DONOVAN, who fumbles under the cover again as KARL strips and gets into bed naked.

DONOVAN: Lights off! Lights off! Hit the lights, man!

KARL turns out the light. Silence.

KARL: Well?

DONOVAN jumps on top of KARL and starts gyrating like a mad dog on heat.

KARL: Easy! Easy! Wait a minute! Isn't you ever heard of foreplay? Huh! Auright...auright...Huh!

DONOVAN: *(Moaning and groaning)* I'm gonna cum!

KARL: What?

DONOVAN:	I'm gonna cum!
KARL:	Don't cum now!
DONOVAN:	I wanna cum.
KARL:	Don't cum! Save it!
DONOVAN:	I have to!
KARL:	You'll fall asleep.
DONOVAN:	I won't!
KARL:	You will.
DONOVAN:	I'll cum again.
KARL:	How long?
DONOVAN:	Half an hour.
KARL:	I don't believe that!
DONOVAN:	How long do you think?
KARL:	Two...three hours...if you wake up at all.
DONOVAN:	Uh! Let me cum. I'm gonna cum. I can cum again!

KARL switches on the light and sits on the edge of the bed.

	What you doing?
KARL:	Let's go back downstairs.
DONOVAN:	What you doing, man? What you let me out for? Turn over.
KARL:	I ain't your woman.
DONOVAN:	Let me go back in.
KARL:	Let go of my arm.
DONOVAN:	You can't do this to me, no, man, please.
KARL:	What's the rush? Got some pussy to see to uptown? Why

	hurry? We've got all night.
DONOVAN:	I couldn't be bothered now.
KARL:	You couldn't be bothered?
DONOVAN:	I couldn't be bothered.
KARL:	Just as well then. *(Rising)* Let's get up.
DONOVAN:	*(Grabs KARL's shoulder)* What's that? Is that bone? *(Giggles)* I could break every bone in your body if I wan'ed. *(Giggles)* Why are you so skinny?
KARL:	Who's skinny?
DONOVAN:	That's bone, man. Never mind! I thought I was skinny. Have you got AIDS?
KARL:	Why? Have you?
DONOVAN:	Serious. Do you always use a condom?
KARL:	I always use a condom.
DONOVAN:	And this bloke last night, you gave it to him, yeah?
KARL:	What are you getting at?
DONOVAN:	You sleep with a lot of white guys, don't you?
KARL:	We've had this conversation.
DONOVAN:	Tell me the truth. You sleep with a lot of white men?
KARL:	None of your business! And if I do, it's probably because I keep meeting jerks like you. Big, dumb, vulnerable Black men with no sense of love for themselves let alone anybody

	else.
DONOVAN:	You think I'm out of order, don't you?
KARL:	I think you're childish, selfish, emotionally immature, sexually retarded and confused.
DONOVAN:	Ah, ah, ah, ah…
KARL:	And if, on top of that, you're trying to say that AIDS is a white man's disease, then you're even more stupid than I thought.
DONOVAN:	Don't call me stupid.
KARL:	White man-made disease or not, Black people are dying of AIDS all over the fucking place - so don't talk crap!
DONOVAN:	Have you got AIDS?
KARL:	If you're so afraid of AIDS, use a condom like the rest of us, or don't have sex. It obviously wouldn't be a great loss to the world.
DONOVAN:	I'm out of order, en I?
KARL:	I know enough Black men living with HIV and AIDS. None to my knowledge have ever slept with White men.
DONOVAN:	Yeah? How old are they?
KARL:	None of your damn business!
DONOVAN:	I'd betta go now, you know. What time is it? Shit! I've forgotten the number. I was

s'ppose to page my friend, but I've forgotten the number. I'd betta get up. Can I use your phone?

DONOVAN gets out of bed, grabs a nearby towel and wraps it around his waist. He dials a telephone number.

Do you think I'm out of order?

KARL:	*(Making bed)* Don't worry about it.
DONOVAN:	No, man, I just couldn't be bothered now.
KARL:	Because you didn't cum or because you think I've got AIDS?
DONOVAN:	I feel all funny now. *(Hangs up phone)* I'll just go to the bathroom. Wash my hands. Make sure I have a bath when I get home. Where's the bathroom? Is there one up here?
KARL:	Straight ahead.
DONOVAN:	Nice.

DONOVAN exits smelling his hands. We hear running water as DONOVAN washes his

**hands in the bathroom.
There is a loud crash as
he drops the soap.**

Shit!

KARL: What's that?

DONOVAN: I dropped the Simple soap.

**KARL makes the bed and
dresses as DONOVAN
enters smelling his
hands.**

KARL: Clean now?

DONOVAN: Safe!

**DONOVAN dresses in
silence. KARL leads the
way downstairs where
they sit as before.**

I s'ppose I'd betta finish my
drink.

KARL: Take the rest with you.

DONOVAN: No, no, man. You have them.
I nicked them, anyway.

KARL: It wouldn't surprise me.

DONOVAN: I used to go to school near
here. I know all this area
really well.

KARL: What school was that?

DONOVAN: Why?

KARL: Just asking.

DONOVAN: I went to Dick Shepherd's.

KARL:	I know Dick Shepherd's.
DONOVAN:	Not really. I went to Forest Hill Boys. Do you know it?
KARL:	I've heard of it.
DONOVAN:	What do you think of it?
KARL:	It's a school like any other school.
DONOVAN:	Useless bunch-a-bastards, en they? I left when I was fifteen.
KARL:	Did you leave or were you asked not to come back?
DONOVAN:	*(Laughing)* No man. Nothing like that. The teachers didn't like us. We used to mess about. Enjoy ourselves. You know how kids are.

<u>KARL looks at him.</u>

No, not really. I was expelled when I was fifteen. Hitting a teacher. Busting his nose. That was two years ago. I'm seventeen now.

<u>KARL looks at him hard, disbelieving.</u>

Don't look it do I? It's cos I'm tired. Sometimes I look a sweet and innocent seventeen. Girls are always coming up to me in clubs and

	saying ... "How old are you? You're really cute aren't you?" Why? How old do I look to you?
KARL:	Twenty-one.
DONOVAN:	I am twenty-one. I look it, don't I?
KARL:	Twenty-one isn't a bad age. Some people think I'm an old man.
DONOVAN:	You?
KARL:	In my shirt and tie, I'm a mature thirty-five.
DONOVAN:	And I'm immature, right?
KARL:	You'd better watch yourself. You might be getting a bit drunk.
DONOVAN:	Are my eyes red?
KARL:	Red as blood.
DONOVAN:	Shit!
KARL:	I think you should go.
DONOVAN:	I used to have really clear eyes once. But that's before I started enjoying myself. I was fifteen at the time. *(Long deep swig)* My parents spent the night with this Black minister. We're Pentecostals, and his son, a right rude bwoy, but very good looking - shared my bedroom. Separate beds, of course. The son was twenty-one. In the night, he strip back his top

sheet and lay in white Y-fronts wanking away right at me. I pretended to sleep but watched it all. He took fifteen minutes to cum. Squirting cream towards me in my bed. Next morning I found him wanking off all over my jeans and he stained the front pure white. He never seem to mind whether I saw him or not, and the room was light enough for me to see him in. He never said a word about it next day at church and I never mentioned it either. But it was very sexy to watch, believe me. *(Swigs)* About a week later, my mate Sticks who was sixteen spent the night by me on the put-you-up-bed. I thought I'd try the same on him. Just after he said "goodnight" I pulled back my quilt and face towards him in his bed. I could see him watching, but he never said a word, breathing heavy, making me think he was asleep.

In the silence, DONOVAN coughs.

KARL:	Is that it?
DONOVAN:	I know it might sound funny to you, me telling it like this, but it turned me on something rotten that I did it whenever I stayed, or friends stayed, overnight.
KARL:	Same room of course.
DONOVAN:	Try it sometime. See what enjoyment you get, or give, to the one who's watching.
KARL:	I think you should go.
DONOVAN:	What? What for? I don't know why I told you, you know.
KARL:	I like it. I do. It's a good story. Pity you couldn't muster up some of that imagination upstairs.
DONOVAN:	I just couldn't be bothered, man. I couldn't be bothered.
KARL:	Hey, my brother, no problem. But what are you still doing sitting here?
DONOVAN:	I don't know, you know. You ask a lot-a-questions.

<u>KARL looks up at him.</u>

	Where's my Poppers?
KARL:	Left-hand pocket.
DONOVAN:	Oh, yeah! Look...what's your name again?
KARL:	What's my name?

DONOVAN:	I've got your number, haven't I? It's on that piece of paper. Shall I give you a call?
KARL:	If you want.
DONOVAN:	See you around, then.
KARL:	See you around.
DONOVAN:	*(off)* You forgot to lock the security gate. You'll lock it now, though.
KARL:	Don't worry!
DONOVAN:	*(off)* Ouch! It's cold out here.

<u>KARL enters and sits as before.</u>

<u>Dim lights to darkness.</u>

Act Two

The kitchen-dining room. One month later. KARL is sorting his washing when the doorbell rings. He goes to the front door:

KARL:	Who is it?
DONOVAN:	*(off)* Me.
KARL:	Who's me?
DONOVAN:	*(off)* Me-me.
KARL:	There are many mes. Who is it? It's late.
DONOVAN:	*(off)* Me.
KARL:	Michael?...
DONOVAN:	*(off)* Don't you know?
KARL:	Look, Michael...it's gone eleven o'clock...
DONOVAN:	*(off)* Why do you keep saying Michael, is he one of your men?
KARL:	Look whoever it is, if you're knocking on my door to talk sensibly to me, then let's talk, okay. If not...
DONOVAN:	*(off)* It's Donovan.
KARL:	Who?
DONOVAN:	*(off)* Donovan from the garage.

KARL:	What garage?
DONOVAN:	*(off)* It's raining out here, man. Can I come in?

**<u>KARL opens the door.
DONOVAN enters.</u>**

	What's up?
KARL:	You alright?
DONOVAN:	I ain't too bad, y'nuh. What's been happening with you?
KARL:	Nothing much.
DONOVAN:	I was just passing.
KARL:	Come in, if you're coming.
DONOVAN:	I saw your lights on, so I...
KARL:	Come in.
DONOVAN:	Cheers, man.
KARL:	Hey, wait a minute. What've you done to your hand?
DONOVAN:	I had a fight jus' now with this bloke outside Brixton loos.
KARL:	Mmm. Stay there. Don't come in yet. I'll get you something to wrap on it. Don't drip blood on my carpet.

**<u>KARL grabs a towel,
runs to the door.</u>**

	Does it hurt?
DONOVAN:	Yeah, I can't move my thumb.

They enter. DONOVAN has the towel wrapped around his hand.

KARL: Wait there a minute.

Exit KARL. DONOVAN looks around. KARL returns with a First-Aid kit, disinfectant, cotton wool, plasters and bandages. He attends to the wound.

DONOVAN: So you cut up your hand? (*Sucks his teeth*) I'm there pissing, fucking idiot comes into the loo staring at my dick. I turn round to him, "What's the matter with you, mate, seen something you like?" "Fucking battieman!" he says. I goes, "Fuck off, cunt! Me nuh want yuh. Me fuck bigger man dan yuh a'ready!"

KARL: That was brave.

DONOVAN: I step outside now the pussy pulls a knife. You shoulda seen him as well, skinny little pop-eyed runt. I nearly killed him.

KARL: You should be careful who

	you're trying to pick up.
DONOVON:	I wasn't pickin' nobody up, man, I was havin' a piss.
KARL:	Those toilets are dangerous.
DONOVAN:	Like I said, I wen' in there to have a piss, okay.
KARL:	How's that?
DONOVAN:	Auright.
KARL:	You might need some stitches.
DONOVAN:	It's just a cut.
KARL:	You should get it seen to anyway. You don't want it to get infected.
DONOVAN:	Don't worry about it.

<u>KARL returns the First-Aid kit. Pause.</u>

	Hey, so what - you guys couldn't stop an' chat the other day when I saw you?
KARL:	We were in a hurry.
DONOVAN:	Oh, yeah?
KARL:	Didn't think you wanted to.
DONOVAN:	Didn't I say hello to you? I said I was gonna check you, didn't I? Where was you going?
KARL:	I was with an American friend. I was taking him out to dinner.
DONOVAN:	What was his name?
KARL:	Wendell.

DONOVAN:	Sounds like a girl.
KARL:	He definitely ain't that.
DONOVAN:	Yeah - so did he enjoy himself ole Wendell?
KARL:	Yes, he did.
DONOVAN:	You showed him a good time?
KARL:	We enjoyed ourselves.
DONOVAN:	So he's gone now?
KARL:	That's right.

Silence.

DONOVAN:	So what you been up to then, Karl, man?
KARL:	Not much.
DONOVAN:	You know I ain't working far from here now.
KARL:	Where's that?
DONOVAN:	Up in Stockwell Park there. That same garage where you saw me.
KARL:	That's a change from the van driving.
DONOVAN:	I'm a good mechanic, man. Thought I'd learn a trade. Well, Susan's idea really.
KARL:	Makes sense.
DONOVAN:	I'm glad you only live round the corner here, though. You know sometimes you don't wanna go home. You never know, our friendship could blossom.

<u>KARL laughs.</u>

	What's the matt'r now?
KARL:	Sorry.
DONOVAN:	No, man, what's funny?
KARL:	You make me laugh.
DONOVAN:	That's what people say. I was always the joker at school...the kid who'd make all the other kids laugh an' get everyone in detention.
KARL:	A disruptive element.
DONOVAN:	A born comedian.

<u>DONOVAN walks around. KARL watches him.</u>

	So, Karl, man, looks like you fixing up the place. Bought some new statues and things. That's nice, man. That's real nice, man. This wood or stone?
KARL:	Wood.
DONOVAN:	I should-a-known, ennit, cos you're into wood. Looks stone to me, though, man. Guy who carved this sure knows his stuff. You never bought these here, though; these must-a-come straight from outta Africa.

KARL:	I went home for a while.
DONOVAN:	That's perceptive of me, ennit?

KARL smiles.

	What you laughing at?
KARL:	Just smiling.
DONOVAN:	It ain't a word you'd expek me to use, is it? Perceptive. I like to surprise people. Like this bloke comes up to me, "Hey, guy, how you feel? " With my hands," I says, "How about you?" I tell you, he creased up. Ha, ha, ha.

KARL laughs too.

	I did, too, cos I surprised myself.
KARL:	*(Mock Texan)* You should-a-been on the stage, kid.
DONOVAN:	Or under it.
KARL:	Don't put yourself down.
DONOVAN:	So what was Africa like, man? What's the people like out there?
KARL:	Poor and clean.
DONOVAN:	Yeah? What part was you in, Guyana?
KARL:	Ghana.
DONOVAN:	That's what I mean, man. Ghana.

KARL:	Yeah, travelled right through the country this time. Normally I just go to see my father, once a year or so, ever since he went back. Then I end up being passed around the family and hanging out with my cousins, chatting up girls I have no interest in, just to belong. Got bored of that. So this time, I travelled from Accra to Paga up North, to the beautiful Lake Bosomtwe, and South, down into the dungeons at Cape Coast.
DONOVAN:	Dungeons?
KARL:	Where the ancestors were kept as slaves.
DONOVAN:	What, they still have 'em?
KARL:	Filled with the moans and the crying of ghosts and the scratches they made on the walls with their fingers. The survivors were herded through a dark, narrow tunnel to the sea and the waiting ship to another hell.
DONOVAN:	Jamaica.
KARL:	Made me sick to the stomach after all these years. But that's me all over, when I don't know a thing, I always like to put myself in

situations that will end my
ignorance, and standing in
that dungeon on the
fossilised shit of my
ancestors, suddenly I could
feel all your pain, and I
understood...

DONOVAN: What?

KARL: Why you are the way you are.
I don't just mean you,
Donovan, I mean, West
Indians. And Africans. The
lot of us. Because we Africans
lost out too. We lost over
forty million of our people.

DONOVAN: You joking?

KARL: Half of those bones at the
bottom of the sea.

DONOVAN: So what the Jews got to
moan about, man?

KARL: You tell me. I couldn't see it
before looking with eyes
only. Now it's made me want
to try harder to connect.

DONOVAN: Did you take any pictures?

KARL: Too pissed off to get them
developed. I just want to get
on the plane and go back.

DONOVAN: I'm gonna have to set foot in
Africa one day. I just know
one day I gotta be there. I
was listening to this bredda
in Hyde Park one time,
chatting about all the things

that unite us.

KARL: If only we could learn to love each other.

DONOVAN: That's the key, ennit, man. *(Sucks his teeth)* Chuh! You wouldn't mind, would you, Karl, if I jus' put these clothes in to wash with yours? My jeans got all blood on 'em.

KARL: Will they dry in time?

DONOVAN: You got a dryer, ain't you? Do you mind?

DONOVAN starts to undress. KARL looks away for fear of revealing his physical attraction, of which DONOVAN is aware, but plays it cool.

Tell you the truth, Karl, man, I been having a bit-a-trouble at home. Susan, y'nuh, the missus. Don't know what's the matter with her, man. Must be something. Maybe it's me. I dunno. Don't wanna bother you or nothin' with my shit, anyway, y'nuh. Ain't been back there since last Sunday. Jus' need a space to think, man. I mean, seen as

	though you can't sleep as well. I was wonderin'; don't wanna keep you up or nothin'...
KARL:	You wouldn't be keeping me up.
DONOVAN:	You sure?
KARL:	Sometimes, I need to get away myself. The sofa turns into a bed.
DONOVAN:	Cheers, man.
KARL:	I'm doing it again.
DONOVAN:	What's that?
KARL:	Nothing.
DONOVAN:	Where do you want these?
KARL:	Just drop them there.
DONOVAN:	Do you mind if I take a shower?
KARL:	*(Points up)* You know where it is.
DONOVAN:	You're a mate, you know that.

DONOVAN sits next to KARL. KARL gets jumpy, gets up, busses himself with washing and tries to fill the uncomfortable silence.

KARL:	People are funny.
DONOVAN:	I know, I was just thinking that.
KARL:	A guy used to come here. I

liked him, nothing like that, met him in the street. We got on well. I took him as a brother. He came here about six weeks ago we sat down one night - drank a few beers, smoked a few joints and chatted. We used up all my weed so he said he'd see me the following day with a draw. But when I woke up the next morning, I couldn't find my wallet. I knew I had when he was here but now it wasn't anywhere. I saw him for the first time yesterday. "Oh, hello, Karl!" he says. I said "Hello!" He says, "How are you?" I said, "I'm fine. Couldn't be better!" Even though I'm sick as a dog for being back in this bloody country. And I expect he was waiting for us to chat. I just walked on. I mean, no quarrel, no argument, nothing, to just steal from the hand of friendship like that. How low down we are. Is it wrong to do good?

DONOVAN: People ain't used to it.

KARL: But if you don't try, how can you ever progress?

DONOVAN: They don't appreciate it,

	Karl, man. You should know that by now.

KARL: That's the trouble with the Blacks in this country. At least in Ghana, we band together. We may still die for the little we want to eat but at least, we have heart. My biggest regret is coming to this country. Because now I might never be able to live in Ghana again, and that scares me.

DONOVAN: Don't worry, man. You'll go back when the time comes. You got any beers?

KARL: None at all.

DONOVAN: *(Sucks his teeth)* I was gonna bring a couple as well. Off-licenses shut now, ennit.

KARL: What's the time?

DONOVAN: Ten past twelve.

KARL: I hate this fucking place - can't even sleep and can't get a fucking drink when you want one.

DONOVAN: What's that up there?

KARL: Cheap American Vodka.

DONOVAN: Vodka?

KARL: Try it. The American brought it.

DONOVAN: What, not that Demetri? You wanna kill me? You can drive a car on that stuff. You

	should-a-told that American to take that shit back with him.
KARL:	I'll have to feed that one to the real winos.
DONOVAN:	The wino children would love you. You don't drive, do you?
KARL:	Love to be driven.
DONOVAN:	You got a bike?
KARL:	Me, no, why?
DONOVAN:	I was gonna nip round this Indian Offie I know...stays open all hours. You should get you'self a mountain bike, man. A bit a pumping does you good.
KARL:	Here bicycle riding is a form of sport. Back home bicycle riding is a sign of poverty.
DONOVAN:	It's jus a different way a seeing things. You miss home, don't you?
KARL:	Missing home now would be like saying I miss hunger. When I can make something good there, then I'll miss home.
DONOVAN:	You've done alright for you'self, though. This place and everything. That's a nice pin you're wearing.
KARL:	It's a badge.
DONOVAN:	Bob Marley, ennit?
KARL:	Peter Tosh.

DONOVAN:	Red, green and gold.
KARL:	The colours of my heart.
DONOVAN:	It's nice, man.
KARL:	This guy came up to me in the airport at Accra, "Oh, my brother, you have returned!", and pinned it on there.
DONOVAN:	Fancy going all the way to Africa and coming back with a Peter Tosh badge.
KARL:	We Ghanaians love our Reggae.
DONOVAN:	How do you know it's not bad luck or something?
KARL:	It's been there ever since and I'm fine.
DONOVAN:	That's nice, though, man. That was a nice thing to do.
KARL:	Some round here would kill you for less.
DONOVAN:	Can I have it?
KARL:	No.
DONOVAN:	Can I wear it for a while?
KARL:	It was given to me.
DONOVAN:	I'll give it back to you.
KARL:	I don't give away things that are given to me.
DONOVAN:	I know, it's not good manners, man, but... Thank you.
KARL:	Don't lose it.
DONOVAN:	It's all the way from Africa.
KARL:	The shower you want is upstairs. I'm going to bed.

DONOVAN:	You gone already?
KARL:	Knock me up if anything exciting happens.

They laugh.

DONOVAN:	You know, you look familiar.
KARL:	You look familiar, too.
DONOVAN:	Must-a-seen you before in one-a-my other life.
KARL:	Good night.
DONOVAN:	See you in the morning.

Exit DONOVAN. KARL puts clothes in the washing machine.

Dim lights to darkness.

Act Three

One month later. We hear the shower running. Maybe a radio plays the news. KARL is writing at the table when the lights come up. More paper balls are scattered at his feet:

KARL:

I can tell a lie from a mile. After a while, you get to know the steely-eyed confidence of a liar. When the person you're going out with, you say to them..."Are you seeing so and so? Are you sleeping with them? Tell me. I won't be upset. I just want to know." When they look you in the face and say "No! Never!" And you know the truth. Because when you knocked to call for your best friend to go swimming - she was obviously too busy. So you looked through the letterbox and you saw your lover's coat hanging on the back of your best friend's door. You get to know a liar when you see one.

DONOVAN enters dressing to go out. He has a shirt in his hand. KARL screws up the piece of paper and throws it at the bin.

	Where's the broom?
DONOVAN:	Leave the cleaning. I'll do it tomorrow.
KARL:	Tomorrow? What's happening tomorrow?
DONOVAN:	I was gonna do...
KARL:	You were going to do what?
DONOVAN:	I was gonna do some spring cleaning.
KARL:	Spring cleaning? What kind of spring cleaning?
DONOVAN:	Oh, Gawd!
KARL:	I never see you touch broom in here before.
DONOVAN:	For fuck sake, man!
KARL:	Don't expect me to do everything round here.

DONOVAN:	I can look after myself.

DONOVAN goes to the fridge and takes a beer.

KARL:	Those are my beers. Not yours.

DONOVAN replaces the beer angrily.

DONOVAN:	What are you playing my music for? Who said you could play my music?

DONOVAN turns the music off. KARL turns it back on.

KARL:	This is the one CD of yours I play.
DONOVAN:	You locked your music up somewhere.
KARL:	I locked my music away because my music was going missing.
DONOVAN:	Well, it's nothing to do with me or my friends.
KARL:	I left the ones you like down here so that you could play them.
DONOVAN:	Just be careful with my things.

KARL:	Tell your girlfriends not to keep ringing this number. You brought your woman into this house.
DONOVAN:	Who told you that?
KARL:	You brought your woman into this house, drinking my drinks, eating my food.
DONOVAN:	Who told you that?
KARL:	Nobody needed to tell me that. The whole place stinks of fish every time.
DONOVAN:	Ahh, naaaw, man, that's nasty. Where'd you get that from?
KARL:	You brought your woman into my house, and you have the nerve to watch dirty videos with her in my bed.
DONOVAN:	Naw, naw, man. It wasn't nothing like that.
KARL:	The videos were all over the place.
DONOVAN:	Look, I gotta go out now, man. My friends are coming to get me any minute now.
KARL:	Did you hear what I said?
DONOVAN:	What?
KARL:	I don't want your girlfriends ringing this house.
DONOVAN:	Safe! Are you watching telly later?
KARL:	I'm watching the telly!
DONOVAN:	I was wondering if...

KARL:	You don't come and tell me that you want to use the dining room.
DONOVAN:	Did I say that?
KARL:	You were going to say that.
DONOVAN:	Forget it, man. Just forget it!
KARL:	I'm taking the television up to the bedroom.
DONOVAN:	It's your telly, ennit.
KARL:	You don't come and tell me at ten minutes to ten that you want to use the dining room.
DONOVAN:	For fuck sake, man. Just cos I'm going out.
KARL:	Ask me if I care.
DONOVAN:	I was gonna ask you, as well, if you wanned to come.

KARL looks at him, silence.

KARL:	We never go anywhere. We never do anything.
DONOVAN:	So why bother then, man?
KARL:	Why did I bother?
DONOVAN:	Yeah?
KARL:	Because ... because I care.
DONOVAN:	We go out.
KARL:	We don't exist, except maybe within these four walls, and that's a bad dream.

DONOVAN:	I'm off now.
KARL:	When are you moving out?
DONOVAN:	When?
KARL:	Date and time? I'm not about to spend another month in this flat with you. I'm going away for a few days, and when I come back, I'm putting the flat on the market.
DONOVAN:	I been doing my homework on Tenant's Rights - it ain't as easy as that.
KARL:	Speak to my Solicitor.
DONOVAN:	I'm speaking to you.
KARL:	Well, I don't want to hear it.
DONOVAN:	But Karl me and you are friends. Just cos I went off with a girl? Sex with a girl is for having babies. She don't mean nothing, man. She's just a girl.
KARL:	And when you have these kids now - what do you do with them? Fuck them off? Leave them to steal and rot and die shooting each other? What kind of love is that?
DONOVAN:	You and me are friends, man. You can't put me out. You know how things stay already

KARL:	Any Sperm Bank can father a child, Donovan. It takes a man to show commitment and love. It takes a man to take responsibility for his own. You'll never know.
DONOVAN:	Cos I'm not a man, is that it? This says I'm a man!
KARL:	Why - was she a good fuck?
DONOVAN:	That's for me to know and for you to find out, ennit. It can't a been a bad one cos she's pregnant.
KARL:	What? *(Pause)* Donovan, you may turn women on with your boyish charm and straight teeth smile, but you can't deliver. You could never deliver. Nice body and everything. But you use people.
DONOVAN:	What?
KARL:	You lie. You manipulate.

<u>DONOVAN chuckles.</u>

Stay there and laugh.

<u>DONOVAN smiles broadly.</u>

DONOVAN:	You're so stupid! *(Pushing KARL)* Don't call me stupid!

KARL:	Excuse me!
DONOVAN:	Don't call me stupid!
KARL:	Excuse me, please.
DONOVAN:	Or else what?
KARL:	Get out of my fucking face!
DONOVAN:	Come on then mister big shot big mouth photographer. You think you know it all. What's all this crap?
KARL:	Put my work down.
DONOVAN:	It's crap!
KARL:	It's my crap. Put it down.

DONOVAN very casually throws the photographs to the floor.

DONOVAN:	Sorry about that.

KARL bends to pick up the photographs and DONOVAN pushes him.

KARL:	Touch me once more, Donovan.
DONOVAN:	What are you gonna do?
KARL:	Once more.

DONOVAN shoves KARL, KARL punches DONOVAN, and they begin to fight. DONOVAN has strength

but KARL'S agility gives him the upper hand. He has DONOVAN in an arm-lock, twisting his hand high behind his back, DONOVAN screams.

KARL:	You were saying?
DONOVAN:	Auright, man, auright! Let me go. You win!
KARL:	Trying to make me look like a fool.
DONOVAN:	I ain't. You win!
KARL:	Damn right, you ain't! On your knees.
DONOVAN:	What?
KARL:	You heard me.
DONOVAN:	No, Karl, man, my new trousers.
KARL:	I won't tell you again.
DONOVAN:	Okay! Okay!
KARL:	You wanna play games? Lick my shoes.
DONOVAN:	No, man, you mad?
KARL:	Lick it!
DONOVAN:	You joking? You joking?
KARL:	You think I'm joking?

KARL yanks DONOVAN'S arm, DONOVAN screams.

Found something you like,
at last- a real man for you.
Lick it, I said!

**<u>DONOVAN licks the
shoe.</u>**

I wanna hear you say "I'm a
big Black Battyman and I
love big Black men." I
wanna hear you say it.
No, man, naw...

<u>The doorbell rings.</u>

DONOVAN: That's my friends them.
Come on, Karl, let me up,
man.

KARL: I wanna hear you say it.

**<u>KARL yanks
DONOVAN'S arm again,
DONOVAN screams.</u>**

DONOVAN: What's the matter with you,
man? You gonna let
everybody know what we're
doing?

**<u>KARL yanks
DONOVAN'S arm again,
DONOVAN shouts:</u>**

I'm a big Black Battyman

and I love big Battymen!

**<u>The doorbell rings
again.</u>**

KARL: Louder!
DONOVAN: I'm a big Black Battyman
and I love big Black men!

**<u>KARL releases
DONOVAN'S arm.</u>**

KARL: That should teach you.
DONOVAN: You nearly broke my arm
off.

**<u>The doorbell rings again
for a long time.</u>**

DONOVAN: Don't answer it!
KARL: It's my door; I'll answer it if
I want.
DONOVAN: I'm not in.
KARL: Oh, fuck off!
DONOVAN: That's them going now
anyway.
KARL: *(Picking up photographs)*
Ask me if I care.
DONOVAN: Yow!

<u>KARL looks at him.</u>

DONOVAN: Undress me. Come on, man.
It's a turn-on. I've never

been undressed before.

KARL:	I forget, everything with you is a first. Ain't you going out?
DONOVAN:	No, man, I'll catch 'em up later. What you saying?
KARL:	Say "Hello!" to Susan for me. Or whatever it is you call your woman. If you change your mind, you know where to find me. I won't be running away.

Exit DONOVAN. KARL turns to the audience:

"*In days 2000 seasons past, our feet roamed freely through golden Ghana soil, our hearts flew up high with birds on a Ghana breeze. You loved me then. Of my tortured enslavement from THE WAY, you must have heard the stories told. I bear some scars but time has changed me none. I love you now as then. Will we meet and love again? Or is our love forever tainted by the historic chain of events since then? I have never lost*

hope completely. Don't you
despair. This Black man
still in search of his
"African" Prince."

KARL goes upstairs to
make the bed. He
undresses and gets into
bed turning the lights
off. Long Pause. Silence.
In the dim moonlight,
DONOVAN appears in
the doorway. He sits on
the bed with bowed
head, then climbs into
bed fully dressed. KARL
wakes.

Donovan? Are you sleeping?
I was thinking, you know,
about the things we said ...
and just the way the whole
relationship is going. And I
think we should ... I'm like
... I really want things to
work out. It's just ... maybe
... Donovan, are you asleep?
What time is it?

No answer. KARL turns

**on the light, pulls back
the covers, DONOVAN
is curled up in bed
crying.**

	Donovan, what's the matter? Dee, babes, please.
DONOVAN:	Don't touch me!
KARL:	Donovan - what's this? What's going on?
DONOVAN:	Just leave me alone.

**Pause, DONOVAN starts
to whimper.**

KARL:	Hey, hey - it's alright. It's alright to cry. Tell me what's wrong.
DONOVAN:	It's nothing.
KARL:	Donovan, please.
DONOVAN:	I went to see Susan. She's in hospital.
KARL:	Susan? Is she okay?
DONOVAN:	She ain't having the baby alright!
KARL:	Oh, Donovan, I'm sorry.
DONOVAN:	The doctors just kept going on at me. Talking, talking, talking. Sat me down and did all kinds-a-test.
KARL:	Tests? What tests?
DONOVAN:	All these big words they kept coming out with. I didn't know anything.

KARL:	What, was it a miscarriage?
DONOVAN:	I didn't know what the fuck they were going on about. They jus' stuck this needle in me and took out my blood.
KARL:	What? What for? What's it got to do with the baby?
DONOVAN:	She's aborting my kid all right! She's got AIDS. Jus' leave me!
KARL:	AIDS?

<u>DONOVAN starts to cry.</u>

	You're all right. You're all right.
DONOVAN:	When AIDS first come out, man, I said, "Boy, I ain't going swimming again."
KARL:	Didn't you and Susan use condoms?
DONOVAN:	She look good, man. She look nice. How was I s'ppose to know?
KARL:	We always use condoms.
DONOVAN:	I'm dying. I feel I'm dying. I've got AIDS, haven't I? It's in my blood. I know I have. Susan gave it to me.
KARL:	Dee, your nose is bleeding.
DONOVAN:	Oh, my God, my nose, it's coming out my nose!
KARL:	Donovan, are you HIV-

	positive?
DONOVAN:	I'm going, man, I'm going.
KARL:	What are you talking about?
DONOVAN:	I'm dirt, man. I'm filth! You don't want nothing to do with me. I'm no good.
KARL:	You're a beautiful Black man. I'll have to keep telling you that because you don't believe me. Do you think I'd let a little thing like this stop us from being together? You don't know me, Dee. I want this relationship.
DONOVAN:	I'm no good.
KARL:	I need you. It's not all gloom, is it? We don't know if you're HIV-positive, do we? You've just got to hang on to the goodness and brilliance, yeah? You've got beautiful eyes, do you know that?

DONOVAN shakes his head.

I like big eyes.

DONOVAN shakes his head again.

I'll call you deer eyes.

DONOVAN:	You're being soppy again

	now.
KARL:	I'll call you Bambi.
DONOVAN:	You're being really soppy again now.
KARL:	I'll be as soppy as I like with you.
DONOVAN:	You're being really...
KARL:	Stay there.

<u>KARL exits to return with a picture of DONOVAN.</u>

KARL:	Look at this picture of you. You look so good when you hold up your head to smile. You should hold your head up to smile more often.
DONOVAN:	You remind me of this Rasta bloke.
KARL:	You've got a thing about Rastas.
DONOVAN:	One day I was with my dad in this pub in Battersea, just after Bob Marley died, and my dad turns round to this Rasta bloke and says, "Now that your God is dead, who you gonna pray to?" And coolly, you know, this Rasta bloke turns to my dad ad says, "We been worshipping him in the flesh. Now we got to worship him in the

spirit." Nobody said another word. He just come over with it cool like. It was the coolness of it. You remind me of him.

KARL helps DONOVAN up; they hug and hold each other tight. KARL slowly removes DONOVAN'S shirt and the belt of his trousers, and then his own clothes. They kiss and hold each other in bed; make love until daybreak; KARL riding DONOVAN, DONOVAN riding KARL; then they fall asleep in each other's arms.

Next morning, DONOVAN wakes first and leaves the room, then KARL wakes.

KARL: Donovan? Donovan? Dee, are you down there? (Gets out of bed, puts on boxer shorts, and exits. Off.) Donovan, are you there?

DONOVAN enters in dressing-gown and sets the table. KARL runs in carrying today's newspaper.

Dee. There you are. I thought you'd left me. I thought you'd decided to call it a day and gone back to Susan.
No. I'm here.

KARL:	Hi!
DONOVAN:	Hi!
KARL:	My mouth taste like the bottom of a sewer, so I won't.
DONOVAN:	So's mine.

They kiss passionately.

DONOVAN:	I'm doing us some breakfast.
KARL:	Good, I'm starving. *(Smiles and looks out the window towards the audience.)* Hello, little birdie-wordie.
DONOVAN:	Where? Oh, yeah. His head's all ruffled. Looks like he's growing locks.
KARL:	*(Broad patois)* Wha'appen, Star?

They laugh.

DONOVAN:	Those birds are really funny. They sit around all day with their mouth wide open waiting for insects to drop in.
KARL:	That's not gonna get them far. Where's this food - I'm starving.
DONOVAN:	It's coming up.
KARL:	No bacon for me. Did I tell you I stop eating pork? A lotta people never touch pork.
DONOVAN:	Unclean meat, man.
KARL:	There're some burgers in the freezer.
DONOVAN:	I'll have to start fattening you up.
KARL:	I burn up a lot of energy.
DONOVAN:	I know you do!
KARL:	It's about time you did some cooking 'round here. You can cook!
DONOVAN:	I like cooking. Fresh, wholesome stuff. I did this course as a Chef once. Then I got bored, man. They wouldn't let me cook anything nice where I was working.
KARL:	I used to hate Cauliflower and things like that.
DONOVAN:	My mum boils vegetables to

	mush. Her carrots dissolve on the plate. Serious, man. Her mushy peas turn liquid green, and everything swimming around in grease and Beef Oxo cube.
KARL:	You shouldn't boil too much of the goodness out.
DONOVAN:	Tell her for me nuh.
KARL:	Your mum sounds nice.
DONOVAN:	She is. We should go up there and see her, you know. She's on her own now. What you smiling at?
KARL:	You.
DONOVAN:	What?
KARL:	The way you were that night we met.
DONOVAN:	Out of order, man. Nothing going on up here. I was at that club again the other night.
KARL:	The Bluenote.
DONOVAN:	Yeah.
KARL:	Haven't been back since. I hear they weren't letting Black people in.
DONOVAN:	They were letting people in - they close the club three hours early. There was this slave on the door.
KARL:	Slave?
DONOVAN:	That's what we call Black guys who only check for

whites.

KARL:	Right!
DONOVAN:	I don't hate white people, you know.
KARL:	I prefer my own myself.
DONOVAN:	That's what it is, ennit? We've got white in our blood anyway.
KARL:	No, *we* haven't!
DONOVAN:	I didn't mean it like that. I mean, me and my family.
KARL:	Oh.
DONOVAN:	You're funny, you are. You get all worked up sometimes. Sometimes I think your heart's too big for your body.
KARL:	I let my feelings show.
DONOVAN:	You should see yourself sometimes, man. Bang out of order!
KARL:	I'm sorry.
DONOVAN:	Naw, man, it's awright! You know where you are, don't you.
KARL:	You don't give much away yourself.
DONOVAN:	I'm like that, though, you know. You say it's cos I don't give. I used to give all the time to people. You ask my mum. But the more I give, the more people want

to take. Take, take, take,
that's all people do. And
then I don't wanna give, cos
I don't wanna feel, and I
don't wanna feel cos I don't
wanna get hurt. Candy hurt
me. Candy my ... we were
gonna get married, man. It's
so stupid. D'you know she
slept with my brother. My
big ole fat ugly brother. If he
was the last man in the
world, I'd rather shag a
sheep. She slept with him to
hurt me. I s'ppose she'd say
she wasn't getting enough.
Trevor hurt me. Trevor was
the first man I met. Trevor
is pathetic! That's one of
your words, ennit? Do you
know he'll swear to God he
screwed me. I overheard
him on the phone one night
showing off to his friend. I
said, "Trevor, you've never
screwed me!" He said, "Yes,
I have!" I said, "When?
Where was I?" D'you know
what I mean? He's so
stupid! I met Nathan right
after Trevor. Nathan was
quite nice at first. Then he
started to want to treat me
like a woman. I wasn't

having none-a-that! I met Susan in Safeways. I thought "I ain't having any luck with men." Susan was really good in bed. "You don't think I'm a slag, do you, Donovan? I'm not a slag, you know. I'm just really really attracted to you!" Susan didn't hurt me. I hurt Susan. She need love, you know. I didn't mean to hurt her. I wanted to have a son. That's what it was. It was mainly to have a kid. How could I love Susan when all the time I was attracted to men? That'll only breed anger and suspicion, ennit? And anyway, here I am now with you - another man - and feeling good about it for the first time in my life. I ain't making no promises to you, Karl. But just to be with you, you know. Talking to another Black man. Someone who can listen without passing judgement. You make me feel so good.

KARL: I love you.

DONOVAN: You an' me then?

KARL: You and me. Where's this

	food?
DONOVAN:	It's coming up, man.
KARL:	We should get some sleep later.
DONOVAN:	I feel like going for a walk, you know, man, but I'm tired too. We didn't get much sleep last night.
KARL:	We didn't use any condoms last night either.
DONOVAN:	I know. How do you feel?
KARL:	I feel fine. How do you feel? I mean, now?
DONOVAN:	You make me feel good, man.
KARL:	We should go to the clinic and get tested. Every three months, or do they say, we should check again.
DONOVAN:	So we can know, if anything.
KARL:	If anything.
DONOVAN:	Yeah.
KARL:	We'll see how it goes. One day at a time. Shall we go up or eat down here?
DONOVAN:	I love you, you know.

KARL smiles, surprised.

I liked you from time, man. It's just me, ennit? Call it progress, if you wanna.

KARL laughs.

DONOVAN laughs too.

Dim lights to blackness.

T H E   E N D

Afterword

Boy with Beer is a love story that tells of the relationship between two Black men. Though certain of that, however, some theatregoers have been inclined to assume the obvious: that the theme is the conflicts/contradictions involved in being both Black and gay. Confronted by racism in society, and heterosexism in their own communities, Black gay men do face formidable challenges, but, in fact, the theme is much broader than that and concerns itself with issues of Black self-love and the power dynamics at the heart of human relationships.

As a play about power, prejudice and the pressures of machismo, about an odd love affair and an extraordinary 'rite of passage,' the struggle of strength in *Boy with Beer* is not just a conflict of men, or of male same-sex relationships, but is a conflict at the centre of any Black love. Particularly in the diaspora where Black men and women have had to be strong,

Black love is almost automatically a competitive dance of strength between strong individuals who must find some level on which to communicate and operate as equals. So often what we find in our heterosexual community, for example, is the Black man who needs a weaker partner, who is not going to confront him on the level of an equal, going for a spouse of another race, where perhaps the women have been taught to be meeker, more subservient, through their history.

As a story about two Black men from different backgrounds, *Boy with Beer* also throws into relief some aspects of the love-hate relationship between Africans and Afro-Caribbean, and between the working class and the upwardly mobile professional class living in Britain today. It investigates some of the social, emotional, political and historical baggage that Black people carry as individuals and collectively. Because Karl is more emotionally and mentally developed than Donovan, we follow his attempts to raise Donovan's consciousness, and how he has to resolve himself in order to share love and understanding with the younger man.

Bar the threat of HIV infection, the ending is ostensibly upbeat- 'and they lived happily ever after.' However, we know in our heart of hearts that there is still more work to be done; for `Mr Right', our ideal mental construct, does not exist except in our own mind's eye, and we must open our hearts to allow him to emerge in the best approximation that destiny has to offer. In this instance, history has conspired to make Black men hate themselves. Yet despite this, Black gay men love each other, can protect, comfort and care for each other in a society that despises 'Blackness', and a Black community that condemns their love. If there is a purity in a love that is as essential as the loving of oneself, then when Black men love each other in an environment that negate them, it is not a sign of sickness - it is a sign of health.

Then, on the other hand, and these are crucial questions for the reader and audience, can Donovan really love Karl and put him at risk of HIV infection? Does Karl really love himself when he foregoes the use of condoms? Is this simply a slice of real life? Or is there some deeper spiritual significance, a reunion of souls after `two thousand seasons past', and a quest for unconditional love that transcends the physical here and now? Is it better for a brother to be prepared to die for a brother or to shoot him in the back with a gun?

Perhaps these musings are purely subjective and find no common ground at all with your own thoughts on the subject. Yet if *Boy with Beer* is nothing more than a simple tale of 'Black gay love' and a call for respect, understanding and dialogue, then I believe it benefits every Black man or woman who sees or reads it, some of whom I hope may see themselves reflected in the characters.

Very special thanks to Topher Campbell, for seeing potential where others saw none; Steven Luckie, for commissioning this extended version of *Boy with Beer* and his dedication to bringing it to the public; and to Tunde Oba and Clive Wedderburn, whom I happen to think are two very special actors.